CONTENTS

WORLD WAR I

World War I broke out on 28 July 1914 and ended on 11 November 1918. It was fought in Europe between two alliances – the Triple Entente (Britain, France, Russia and others) and the Triple Alliance (Germany, Austria-Hungary and others). As in all wars, each side needed to keep secrets to gain advantages over the enemy. These included plans of attack, secret weapons and secret missions. And at the same time both sides tried to discover the enemy's secrets, using spies and code-breakers.

The manufacture of ammunition was part of the arms race that led up to World War I.

THE BUILD-UP TO WAR

Between the 1870s and the beginning of World War I, the major countries of Europe were Britain, France, Germany, Austria-Hungary and Russia. Over the years these countries formed various alliances, promising to support each other if one or the other was attacked. By 1907 Britain, France and Russia were

RIVAL NATIONS IN 1914

France was keen to win back from Germany land it had lost in the Franco-Prussian War (1870–1871). It was also nervous of German power. **Britain** had a vast empire and the biggest navy, but it was also worried about Germany's growing strength. **Germany** wanted to increase its influence around the world and gain territory. This aggressive policy worried the other nations. **Russia**, the largest European state, wanted to expand. **Austria-Hungary** had an empire that covered a vast area of central Europe.

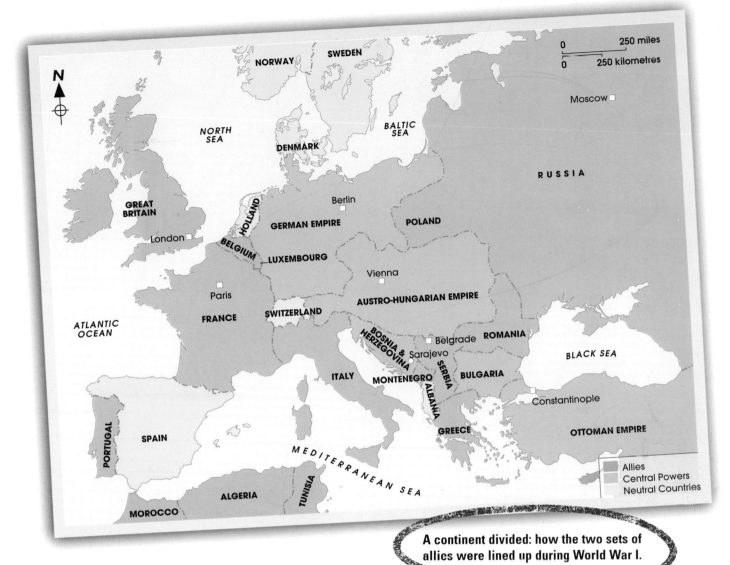

A continent divided: how the two sets of allies were lined up during World War I.

allies, forming the Triple Entente, or Allied Powers. Germany had an alliance with Austria-Hungary and Italy, known as the Triple Alliance, or Central Powers.

ARMS RACE

The countries began an arms race, manufacturing guns and building warships. By 1914 the alliances were prepared for battle against each other. All that was needed was a spark to ignite a war. That spark was the assassination of Archduke Franz Ferdinand, heir to the throne of Austria-Hungary (see page 8).

ITALY'S SECRET PACT

In 1914 Italy was part of the Triple Alliance. When World War I started it should have helped Germany and Austria-Hungary, but it didn't. A few months later, Italy entered a secret agreement to join the Allied Powers later in the war. In 1915 the Italians signed another secret agreement to join the war in exchange for land if the war was won by the Allies.

WAR BREAKS OUT

World War I began in the Balkans, parts of which were controlled by Austria-Hungary. The people here wanted independence from Austria-Hungary. In addition, one of the Balkan countries, Serbia, wanted to take land from Austria-Hungary. Austria-Hungary was nervous about Serbian power and was determined to attack Serbia. Germany promised to support Austria-Hungary if it did. But Russia promised to support Serbia.

ASSASSINATION IN SARAJEVO

Seven members of the Black Hand (see page 9) travelled undercover to Sarajevo, Bosnia, to kill Archduke Franz Ferdinand. They positioned themselves along the route the archduke's car was due to take. One threw a grenade, but it exploded under the wrong car, injuring some of the archduke's staff. Later, as the archduke was travelling to hospital to see the injured, another of the gang, Gavrilo Princip, stepped forwards and shot the archduke and his wife.

The spark that started the war: Serbian activist Gavrilo Princip shoots and kills Archduke Ferdinand of Austria-Hungary and his wife in Sarajevo.

SECRET FORCES

In 1912 a handful of Serbians formed a secret group called the Black Hand to support Serbs in Austria-Hungary. The Black Hand planned and carried out terrorist attacks in Austria-Hungary. On 28 June 1914 a Black Hand activist shot dead Archduke Franz Ferdinand, heir to the throne of Austria-Hungary.

CONSEQUENCES

Austria-Hungary demanded that Serbia allow police from Austria-Hungary to investigate the assassination plot. Serbia rejected the demands, and Austria-Hungary declared war on Serbia on 28 July 1914. Within days, the Russians began preparing for war on Austria-Hungary. Germany declared war on Russia and then on France. German troops marched into Belgium, aiming to invade France. Britain then declared war on Germany.

THE TRENCHES

In the first weeks of the war German forces made quick advances on two fronts, against both France and Russia.

British troops go 'over the top' during the Battle of the Somme in 1916. Their chances of survival were slim.

But soon they ground to a halt. On both fronts the sides dug in, creating lines of defensive trenches that hardly moved for the rest of the war. Conditions for the soldiers in the trenches were appalling.

IN THEIR OWN WORDS

My first spell in the line [trenches] lasted three weeks. Water was scarce, and even the tea ration was so short there was none left over for shaving. I had a nine days' growth of beard when we went down to rest. My socks were embedded in my feet with caked mud and filth and had to be removed with a knife.

Private Harold Saunders, British Army, 1916

GERMAN SPIES IN BRITAIN

Germany began spying on Britain several years before World War I began. The German secret service organized a network of spies (known as a spy ring) in Britain, mainly to gather information about the British navy and its ships. The German spies were controlled from Germany by Gustav Steinhauer, a naval intelligence officer. He wrote to the spies in Britain under the name of Mrs Reimer.

The fate of many captured spies, such as this unfortunate German, was death by firing squad.

BLENDING IN

Some recruits to the German spy ring were Germans already living in Britain. Some were even British citizens. They had jobs and houses and lived normal lives. One such spy was Karl Gustav Ernst, a London hairdresser. He was arrested on the first day of the war, after the police intercepted his messages to the German secret service about ship movements.

IMAGINED SPIES

When the first German spies were discovered, spy fever swept Britain, and the public, encouraged by the newspapers, became paranoid. Thousands of innocent people with German or Austrian names or connections became suspects. Many people demanded that all Germans in Britain should be deported.

Other spies travelled to Britain from Germany on false or non-German passports. Carl Hans Lody was one. He spoke perfect English, had an American passport and volunteered to spy on the British naval fleet. Lody was captured in Ireland after letters he sent in German were discovered.

LACK OF RESULTS

Most German spies were poorly trained, and in the end they did little to help Germany. Sometimes they sent home misleading reports. In early 1914, while they tried to spy on British naval installations, they failed to notice the build-up of the British expeditionary force that was being prepared to defend France.

FRITZ JOUBERT DUQUESNE

Duquesne was a South African who hated Britain because of British policies in South Africa. In 1914, while in Brazil, he planted bombs on British ships. In 1916 he disguised himself as a Russian duke and joined the British Secretary of State for War, Field Marshal Horatio Herbert Kitchener, on HMS *Hampshire*. On the way from Britain to Russia, Duquesne secretly signalled to a German U-boat, which then sank the *Hampshire*. Nearly all on board drowned, Kitchener included, but Duquesne escaped.

World War I spy, saboteur and assassin Fritz (or Frederick) Joubert Duquesne. This photograph was taken decades later, during World War II, when he was arrested by the FBI for spying in the United States.

INVISIBLE MESSAGES TO GERMANY

The agents of the German spy ring in Britain used various methods of getting information back to Germany. They sent innocent-looking telegrams and letters that contained secret code words. They sometimes sent messages by homing pigeon. Secret ink was very popular. Spies used secret ink to write invisible messages on documents such as letters, pictures and even sheet music that they sent to Germany.

Carrier pigeons, here used by British soldiers, carried messages back to their 'home' roosts.

MULLER'S SECRET MESSAGES

Carl Muller was a German agent who arrived in London in 1915. He wrote letters in English to other agents to be passed on to his spymasters in Germany. Between the lines of English he wrote secret messages in invisible ink made from lemon juice. Muller was suspected of being a spy and his letters were intercepted and the messages discovered. He was tried and sentenced to death.

DISAPPEARING INK

Simple invisible inks include lemon juice and onion juice. Writing made in these liquids disappears when it dries. But when the paper is heated, the ink becomes brown and the writing shows up. Other inks are made from chemicals. They are revealed when the paper they are on is treated with certain other chemicals.

One of the invisible-ink letters sent from England by German spy Courtney de Rysbach. The message (now revealed) was written in invisible ink between the lines of the musical score. You can read what it said below.

MUSIC HALL SPY

Courtney de Rysbach was a popular music-hall entertainer in Britain, and also a German spy. He sent messages to Germany written in invisible ink in the spaces between the notes on sheet music. His secret ink was made from toothpaste mixed with a chemical called potassium ferrocyanide. It was revealed by treating the paper with ferric chloride solution, which made the ink show up in blue. In 1915 the British intercepted one of Rysbach's letters and found its secret message. Rysbach was arrested.

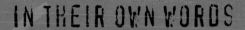

IN THEIR OWN WORDS

The message from Rysbach that was intercepted by the British read as follows:

If you could only send me some money I could get my brother who is in the Navy to give me all the Navy movements, he could be most valuable but he would want money for it…. I will send you a telegram with my new name and address please telegraph me the money it is safer! The newspaper trick is found out and very carefully watched.

Message to Germany from Courtney de Rysbach

BLACK TOM

The United States was a neutral country before it entered the war in 1917. But it did sell arms and ammunition to the Allied Powers. So German spies began operating in the United States. They reported back on the movement of shipping to Europe and attempted to sabotage the supply chain for arms. Their most famous act was the destruction of Black Tom.

GERMAN PLOTS

German spies hatched several secret plots in the United States. They made small, time-delayed 'pencil' bombs that sank supply ships travelling to Europe. They tried to divert explosive-making chemicals away from American ammunitions factories – a plan known as the Great Phenol Plot. And they attempted (but failed) to kill livestock on American farms by injecting them with the deadly germ anthrax.

Firefighters hose down the mangled remains of the Black Tom ammunitions depot near New York, destroyed by German saboteurs.

WEAPONS STORE

Black Tom was an ammunitions depot on the coast of New Jersey, just a few kilometres from New York City. The depot was the size of 30 football pitches and was covered with ammunition – artillery

shells, gunpowder and small arms ammunition. There were millions of tonnes of it, all waiting to be shipped to British, French and Russian forces in Europe.

HUGE EXPLOSION

In the early hours of 29 July 1916, Lothar Witzke and Kurt Jahnke, two veterans of the German spy ring, rowed a boat to Black Tom and planted bombs. At 2.08 am the bombs set off a massive blast. The shock wave broke windows many kilometres away and made bridges and tall buildings sway. Fires started and more explosions followed. By the morning Black Tom had all but disappeared

SABOTAGE

The Americans discovered that the disaster was not an accident, but an act of sabotage. Public opinion in the United States began to turn against Germany, and the attack on Black Tom was one of the reasons why the United States entered the war.

THE END OF THE LINE

Other attacks followed Black Tom, and more were planned. But then German spy Heinrich Albert made a mistake. One day he left his suitcase on a New York subway train, and it was handed into the police. The case contained plans for further secret operations. The Americans were furious and began to crack down on German spies. Albert was arrested and deported.

BRITISH COUNTER-ESPIONAGE

In the years leading up to World War I, the British government became increasingly worried about a German spy ring operating in Britain. They were especially concerned about the Germans finding out about new British naval ships and weapons. So in 1909 the British created the Secret Service Bureau to track down the spies.

Sir Vernon George Waldergrave Kell, head of British counter-espionage during World War I.

LEADERS AND NAMES

Two men, Captain Vernon Kell of the army and Captain Mansfield Cumming of the navy, were put in charge of the Secret Service Bureau. The new organization was soon asked to handle British spying abroad, too, and so was split into two sections. Kell – secretly known as 'K' –

OUT OF HARM'S WAY

When war broke out, there were thousands of German and Austrian people living in Britain. Most were not spies, but all were under suspicion and given a new status as 'enemy aliens'. Some were deported, some were locked up and some were prevented from travelling until war ended in 1918.

German nationals in London wait to be deported to Germany following the outbreak of war.

took charge of the counter-espionage section. Cumming led the foreign section (see page 18). In 1916 the counter-espionage section was given its own name – the Security Service, or MI5 (short for Military Intelligence section 5), the name it still uses today.

AGENT ACTIVITIES

After two years, the Secret Service Bureau had arrested nobody. But gradually, through hard work and a little luck, they identified a few suspects. Some suspects were arrested, but others were watched in case they led the bureau's agents to more spies. All the suspected spies were arrested when war broke out. This dealt a serious blow to German espionage, but it didn't stop it.

BREAKING THE SPY RING

In 1911, by chance, a Secret Service Bureau agent overheard two Germans on a train talking about letters from home. The men were tracked, and the letters turned out to be orders for spies from German intelligence. British agents secretly intercepted later letters, which led them to many other suspects. One of these was Karl Gustav Ernst, who acted as a 'post box'. On 4 August 1914, the day Britain declared war, Kell's agents were ready to pounce. A total of 21 suspected spies were arrested across Britain, including Ernst. Of these, 13 were found to be German agents.

ALLIED SPIES

The foreign section of the British Secret Service Bureau (see page 17) was in charge of spying on Germany and Austria-Hungary. The British were especially interested in the activities of the German navy. Britain had the upper hand on the seas, and it wanted to keep it that way. The section was led by Captain Mansfield Cumming – known in the organization as 'C'. In 1916 it was renamed the Secret Intelligence Service, or MI6 (short for Military Intelligence section 6).

SPIES IN PALESTINE

British spying activities were not restricted to Europe. Spies also operated in the Middle East and India. Palestine was under the control of the Ottoman, or Turkish, Empire, which had entered the war in 1914 on the side of the Central Powers. Some Jews in Palestine formed a spying network called Nili. From 1916 Nili supplied information to the British about Turkish forces, defences and supply lines. Information from Nili helped the British make a surprise attack on the Turks in Palestine that eventually led to a Turkish surrender.

Spies helped in the capture of Jerusalem by the British in 1917. Here, General Allenby, head of British forces in Palestine, enters the city.

ALFRED REDL

Austrian army officer Alfred Redl was head of the counter-espionage service in Austria-Hungary. But he was actually a double agent working for the Russians. He gave most of Austria-Hungary's military secrets away, and he betrayed Austrian spies who were operating in Russia. Russia used the information to its advantage when it attacked Austria-Hungary in 1914. When Redl's activities were discovered in 1913, he killed himself.

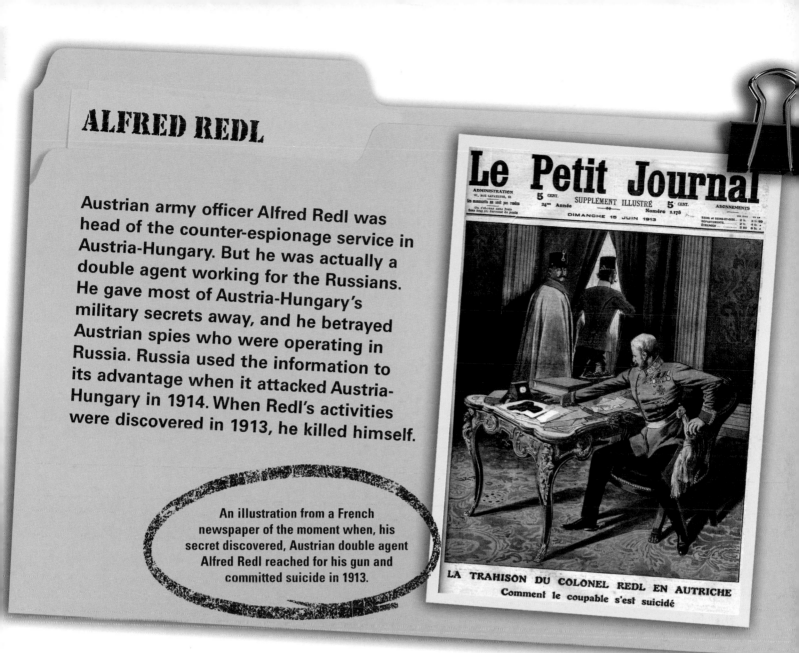

Le Petit Journal

DIMANCHE 15 JUIN 1913

LA TRAHISON DU COLONEL REDL EN AUTRICHE
Comment le coupable s'est suicidé

An illustration from a French newspaper of the moment when, his secret discovered, Austrian double agent Alfred Redl reached for his gun and committed suicide in 1913.

NEW AND OLD TECHNOLOGY

From 1909 Cumming organized part-time agents in Germany to watch German naval shipyards. Hundreds of his spies operated behind the German lines in France and Belgium. They secretly sent back useful information about German troop, artillery and aircraft movements by homing pigeon and by balloon. However, Cumming's attempt to build up a network of spies in Germany itself was unsuccessful.

LETTERS HOME

Britain's intelligence was not limited to trained spies. British soldier Conrad O'Brien-Ffrench was wounded and captured in August 1914. He spent the war in a POW camp, where he gathered information about German troops from new prisoners and sent it home in personal letters using invisible ink.

FEMALE SPIES

At the battle front the war was dominated by men, but women played important roles in espionage. These included Edith Cavell and Mata Hari, who is perhaps the most famous woman spy ever.

GERTRUDE BELL

Gertrude Bell was a British woman who studied history and archaeology, learned several languages, including Arabic, and travelled widely in Europe and the Middle East. She was recruited by British intelligence to provide information about the Arabs and to encourage an Arab revolt against the Turks.

The famous Dutch double agent and dancer Mata Hari. She worked for the French, but spied for the Germans.

MATA HARI

Margarethe Zelle was born in Holland in 1876. In her twenties she made a living as a dancer, using the stage name Mata Hari. She toured Europe and became famous. Around 1903 a German spymaster who saw her act thought she would make a good spy and put her through spy school. She was in Paris when the war started. There she met a French intelligence officer who also thought she might be a good spy. So she became a double agent. But the French eventually suspected her of working for the Germans. In 1917 she was arrested and executed by firing squad.

EDITH CAVELL

Englishwoman Edith Cavell was matron of Berkendael Medical Institute in Brussels, Belgium. After Brussels was captured by the Germans in 1914, she helped British, French and Belgian soldiers trapped behind enemy lines to escape into Holland. She calmly hid the soldiers in her house at the Institute, and gave them clothes, food and money for their journeys. Other Belgians helped Cavell look after and guide the soldiers. Over the following year she helped more than 200 soldiers escape. Her luck ran out in August 1915. She was arrested by the German authorities and later executed by firing squad.

British nurse Edith Cavell helped hundreds of Allied soldiers escape from behind enemy lines.

A GERMAN MISTAKE

Edith Cavell's execution backfired against Germany. People accepted that she was guilty, but they thought that executing her was an act of murder, and she became a martyr. In Britain, propaganda posters, books and newspaper articles were published about her, denouncing the Germans as devils. For the next two months, the number of men who volunteered for military service doubled.

IN THEIR OWN WORDS

Nothing but physical impossibility, lack of space or lack of money, would make me close my house to Allied fugitives.

Edith Cavell

CODES AND CIPHERS

Codes and ciphers are ways of making messages secret, so that only a person who knows what the code or cipher is can read them. Codes and ciphers are vital in war to keep communications secret from the enemy. In World War I they were more important than ever before, due to the development of radio. They were used at the battle front to communicate with naval ships and submarines, and for the governments of different countries to talk to each other.

CODE OR CIPHER?

In a code, different words or phrases in a message are changed into groups of letters, numbers, signs and even sounds. For example, XY might stand for tank, and YX for ship. A code book is needed to code and decode the messages. In a cipher, each letter in the message is changed into a different letter or group of letters. For example, in a very simple cipher, each letter might be changed for the next one in the alphabet.

A German telephone station set up in a wood during World War I.

HOW MESSAGES WERE SENT

Messages were sent by hand, along telegraph wires, by telephone and by radio – World War I was the first war in which radio played a major role. Messages were encrypted when there was a chance that the enemy could listen in. This was the case with messages sent over telegraph or telephone lines, because these were regularly tapped by the enemy. Messages sent by radio also had to be encrypted, because anybody with a radio set could be listening in.

KEEPING AHEAD OF THE CODE-BREAKERS

Of course, each side tried to decode or decipher messages they intercepted (see pages 24–25 for more on code-breaking). As codes and ciphers were broken, new, more complex ones were invented. And for security, codes and ciphers, and the radio frequencies they were transmitted on, were changed regularly.

THE ADFGX CIPHER

In 1918 the Germans introduced a new cipher system known as ADFGX. Each letter in the message was changed to a pair of letters, but only using the letters ADFGX. These letters were used because they are easy to distinguish from each other in Morse code, so that fewer mistakes would be made:

Step 1:
Letters of the alphabet were placed in a grid:

	A	D	F	G	X
A	f	z	t	n	i/j
D	g	l	d	s	b
F	y	v	p	e	a
G	k	c	u	w	r
X	o	m	x	q	h

Each letter in the message was substituted with a two-letter code from the table. So the word 'secret' became:

DGFGGDGXFGAF

Step 2:
This text was written in rows under a keyword (e.g. WAR), and the columns were then exchanged to put the keyword in alphabetical order:

WAR	ARW
DGF	GFD
GGD	GDG
GXF	XFG
GAF	AFG

Then the columns were written down in order to make the final message:

GGXAFDFFDGGG

CODE-BREAKERS

The amount of radio communications grew quickly during World War I. First, radio was used to send telegraphs, and later telephone calls. Because radio communications were easy to listen into, a vast number of messages were intercepted. So a new specialized form of military intelligence began – signals intelligence. Its job was to listen into enemy radio communications, break codes and ciphers, and pass useful information to the generals in charge.

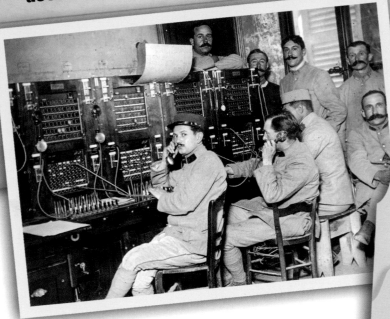

The central telephone switchboard of the Allies in Aisne, France, in 1916. The soldiers are monitoring the lines for sounds of telephone tapping by the enemy.

IDEAS IN THE BATH

Dilwyn Knox, known to his friends as 'Dilly', was one of the best 'Room 40' code-breakers. He found that he could think clearly about breaking new codes while he was sitting in the bath at home. So he ordered a bath that he could sit in at work, too.

ROOM 40

Code-breaking was not an easy job. Codes were very tough to break, and ciphers could be very complicated. The code-breakers were often expert mathematicians who could identify patterns in the scrambled messages.

Soon after the start of the war, the British set up a specialist code-breaking section. It was based in Room 40 of an Admiralty building in London, and so became known as the 'Room 40' group. In 1917 'Room 40' made one of the most famous code-breaking discoveries of all time, known as the Zimmerman Telegram (see pages 38–39).

THE MAGDEBURG CODE BOOK

During World War I, navies used code books for radio communications because codes were safer than ciphers. In August 1914 the German light cruiser *Magdeburg* ran aground in a battle with the Russians. Most of the code books on board were destroyed, but unknown to the Germans, three were captured. The Russians gave one to the British, who were then able to decode German naval messages.

The German cruiser *Magdeburg*, from which German naval code books were captured in 1914.

GEORGES PAINVIN

The French operated a Cipher Bureau staffed by code-breakers. Some were brilliant at the job. They included Lieutenant Georges Painvin. He was given the job of cracking the German ADFGX cipher (see page 23), which the Germans thought was unbreakable. After months of work, Painvin was able to decipher a few messages, which gave the Allies some help in fighting off a German offensive in 1918.

THE CODE TALKERS

The Americans found that their telegraph and telephone messages, both over land lines and radio, were being intercepted and decoded by the Germans. It made it almost impossible for them to operate at the front – the Germans seemed to know their every move. They tried using messengers (called runners) to carry messages, but this was slow and many runners were killed or captured. Another problem was that coding and decoding messages took up valuable time in the heat of battle. Something new was needed – and the solution came in the form of Native Americans.

NATIVE AMERICANS IN WORLD WAR I

When the United States entered the war in 1917, Native Americans were not allowed to be US citizens. In fact, they were not allowed to vote in elections until 1924. Despite this, more than 10,000 Native Americans served in the US Army in World War I.

Native Americans on board a mocked-up naval ship in Manhattan, New York, where they are being encouraged to join the US Army and fight in World War I.

MANY DIFFERENT LANGUAGES

The Native Americans are the native peoples of North America. There are many different Native American tribes, each with their own language. Thousands of Native Americans served in the US Army, and at some point somebody realized that Native American languages might be used for secret communications over the telephone. It was extremely unlikely that any Germans listening in would be able to understand a single word.

A member of the Choctaw tribe dances for tourists in Phoenix, USA. The tourists may be unaware of the vital part his ancestors played in World War I.

THE CHOCTAW TRIBE

Eight soldiers from the Choctaw tribe were chosen to be the first 'code talkers'. To send a message, one Choctaw would translate the message into his language and speak the message down the telephone to another Choctaw, who would translate it back into English. The Choctaws were first used in October 1917, allowing American soldiers to make a surprise attack on German positions. The Choctaw code talkers played an important role in turning back a major German offensive in 1918. Later, German officers admitted that their telephone tapping was rendered useless by the Choctaws.

CHOCTAW CODES

The Choctaw language did not have words for military items such as artillery or machine gun, so the code talkers had to improvise. For example, for 'artillery' they used Choctaw for 'big gun', and for 'machine gun' they used Choctaw for 'little gun shoot fast'.

SECRET WEAPONS IN BATTLE

To advance, troops had to cross no-man's land towards enemy trenches, an act that was normally suicidal because of enemy machine-gun fire. The result was deadlock, with neither side being able to move forward. So both the Allies and the Central Powers secretly developed weapons that would give them the edge.

American soldiers stage a pretend gas attack, to show the lethal consequences of forgetting to put on a gas mask.

GAS WARFARE

Military leaders on both sides in World War I used deadly gas to weaken or kill enemy troops before an advance. The Germans used it first. In April 1915, near Ypres, Belgium, they released chlorine gas from canisters in front of their trenches. The gas formed a yellow-green cloud that drifted towards French positions. The French thought it was simply a smoke

IN THEIR OWN WORDS

Plainly something terrible was happening. What was it? Officers, and Staff officers too, stood gazing at the scene, awestruck and dumbfounded; for in the northerly breeze there came a pungent nauseating smell that tickled the throat and made our eyes smart.

Anothony Hassack, British Army, first gas attack, April 1915

screen and stayed put, preparing for a German advance. When the gas arrived, the French soldiers began to choke, and then fled from their positions.

After this, the British and French felt justified in using gas themselves. During the war, both sides developed new types of gas, and thousands died in gas attacks.

SITTING DUCKS

Early tanks were slow and unreliable. Most broke down and became sitting ducks. But the British persevered, and success came with the first mass tank attack in November 1917, when 476 tanks swept through the German lines at the Battle of Cambrai.

SWINTON'S LANDSHIP

Ernest Swinton was a British army press reporter, who was horrified to see how easily British troops were cut down by machine guns. He realized the army needed a machine like a tractor, but armoured and on tracks, that could reach the enemy lines. His idea was dubbed the 'landship'. The prototype, now called a tank, was demonstrated in September 1915. Then, in great secrecy, the British began manufacturing their Mark I tank. The Germans were very surprised when tanks first lumbered into battle in September 1916.

SECRET WEAPONS IN THE AIR

World War I was the first war in which aircraft were widely used as a weapon. Even the best aircraft were slow and cumbersome, but military leaders could see their potential for spying on the enemy. As the war progressed, each side secretly developed faster, better aircraft. If an aircraft landed or crashed behind enemy lines, it was examined carefully to see if it was carrying any new technology that could be copied.

Observation balloons like this German one were used to gain a good viewpoint over the trenches.

TRENCH GAMES

On the ground, troops tried to deceive the crews of reconnaissance aircraft. They built dummy trenches and dressed them to look occupied. They also hid whenever aircraft came over so that their trenches looked empty.

SPIES IN THE SKY

Pilots flew reconnaissance missions over enemy lines to try and see enemy troop and artillery positions. The pilots or their observers made sketches and notes, and took photographs. They used their radios to pass on any urgent information.

An aircraft gunner aims his machine gun. In single-seat fighters, secret systems were developed to allow the pilot to shoot forwards, through his propeller.

FIRING FORWARDS

In the first single-seat fighters, the pilot had to fire sideways at enemy aircraft. He couldn't fire forwards because he would have shot away his own propeller. This problem was solved by French aviator Roland Garros in April 1915. He added metal deflector plates to his propeller blades, which stopped bullets from damaging them. This secret system gave Garros a huge advantage – he could fire at an aircraft he was chasing. But then disaster struck: Garros was forced to land behind German lines, and the secret was out.

The Germans took the idea a step further. They designed a synchronized machine gun. It had a mechanism that prevented the gun from firing when a propeller blade was in line with the gun.

PLANES WITH NO PILOT

Pilotless planes were experimented with during World War I. In the United States, Elmer Sperry designed a radio-guided flying bomb, which he called an aerial torpedo. It made some promising test flights, and one American admiral thought it might be used to attack German submarine bases. But development was too slow for it to be used in the war. The French sometimes used unmanned gliders made from old fighters as flying bombs. The gliders were given a dummy pilot and an explosive charge and then released over enemy lines.

SUBMARINE WARFARE

Submarines fought a secret battle, hiding below the waves to creep up on enemy ships and then make surprise attacks. Both sides used submarines, but the Germans used them most effectively.

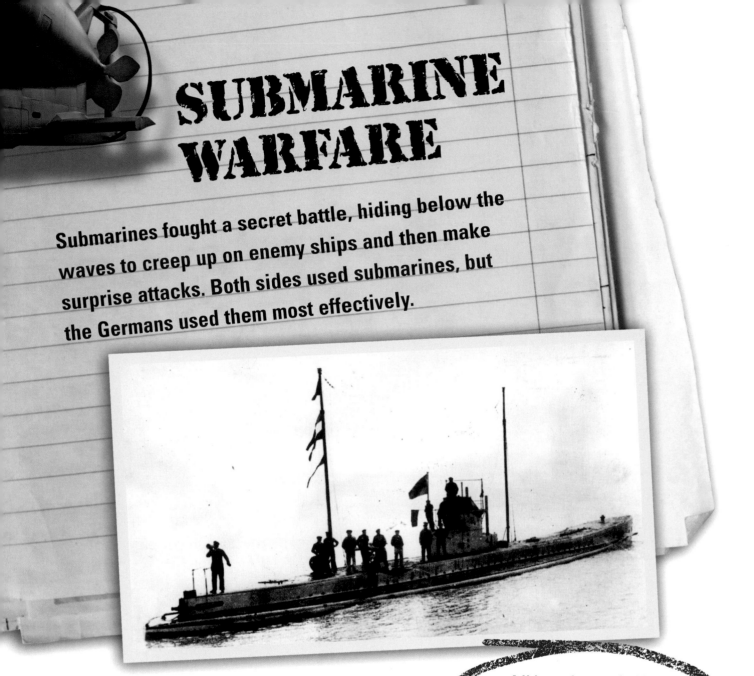

U-BOATS

Germany had a small fleet of submarines, or 'U-boats', when war was declared, but quickly built more. Their first success was the sinking of the British ship HMS *Pathfinder* with a torpedo in September 1914. In the first six months of the war the U-boats attacked only naval ships, but in February 1915 they began what was called 'unrestricted submarine warfare'.

A U-boat, photographed in 1916. The Germans built 360 U-boats during the war, and they sank over 11 million tonnes of shipping.

This meant they attacked unarmed merchant ships too, often without warning. The German plan was to prevent food and military supplies from reaching Britain. U-boats sank nearly 5,000 ships during the war. But 178 U-boats were lost.

THE LUSITANIA

On 7 May 1915 the U-20 sank the British ocean liner *Lusitania*. The ship was travelling from the United States to Britain, and 1,198 passengers died, including 128 Americans. The sinking caused outrage in the United States. Strong protests from the Americans put a stop to U-boat attacks on merchant ships.

Life boats are rowed away as the liner *Lusitania* goes down, critically damaged by a torpedo from a U-boat.

Q-SHIPS

To fight back against the U-boats, the British converted some small merchant ships into decoy ships. The ships had torpedoes and guns hidden by secret doors and panels. The ships became known as Q-ships. Old and untidy ships were deliberately chosen for the job. U-boats didn't waste valuable torpedoes on ships like this – they surfaced and sank them with their deck guns.

The first success came in July 1915. U-36 surfaced and approached the apparently defenceless merchant ship *Prince Charles*. As the U-boat prepared to attack, the crew of the *Prince Charles* threw open their secret panels and fired, sinking U-36. Eventually the U-boat crews learned about the Q-ship trick, but Q-ships sank a total of 14 U-boats and damaged dozens more.

IN THEIR OWN WORDS

I travelled on the surface except when we sighted vessels, and then I submerged, not even showing my periscope, except when it was necessary to take bearings. It was ten minutes after six on the morning of last Tuesday when I caught sight of one of the big cruisers of the enemy.

Otto Weddigen, Commander, U-9, September 1914

TUNNELLING UNDER THE TRENCHES

Some soldiers were diggers whose job was to dig secret tunnels under no-man's land and plant mines under the enemy trenches. When the tunnellers were sure they were right under the enemy trenches, they filled the end of a tunnel with explosives and then blocked up the tunnel with sand bags. They laid wires to detonators in the explosives so they could set off the explosives from the safety of their own trenches.

DIRTY, DANGEROUS WORK

The tunnellers were often ex-miners, who were expert diggers and knew how to support tunnel roofs. They dug down from behind their own trenches and then out under no-man's land. It could take them many months to reach the enemy. The tunnellers had to keep as quiet as they could as they dug because the enemy was listening for them. And tunnels dug by opposite sides could pass within a few metres of each other. Sometimes they broke through, and there was hand-to-hand fighting underground. The tunnellers' job was dirty, dangerous and often terrifying. Tunnels regularly collapsed.

French tunnel diggers, or 'sappers', at the entrance to a tunnel they were digging towards enemy lines on the Western Front in July 1916.

34

THE BIGGEST BLAST

As the war progressed, the mines planted by the tunnellers became larger and more destructive. In January 1917 British tunnellers began secretly digging towards the German lines near the village of Messines, Belgium. They dug eight kilometres of tunnels and planted 19 enormous mines under the German trenches. The mines were detonated on 7 June at the start of the Battle of Messines. It's estimated that 10,000 soldiers were killed in an explosion so large that it was heard in London, 230 kilometres away.

DISCOVERING TUNNELS

Soldiers in the trenches were always listening for enemy tunnellers below. One method they used was to push a stick into the ground and rest their teeth on top, so they could feel vibrations caused by digging. Another was to half-bury an oil drum full of water into the bottom of a trench, and then put an ear in the water to listen for digging sounds. Tunnellers also dug 'counter tunnels' to try to find enemy tunnels.

Wires were laid from underground mines back to the trenches. Here, a German officer prepares to detonate a mine under Allied trenches.

IN THEIR OWN WORDS

A soldier describes the huge explosion at the start of the Battle of Messines:

In front the earth opened and a large black mass was carried to the sky on pillars of fire, and there seemed to remain suspended for some seconds while the awful red glare lit up the surrounding desolation.

Private Gladden, British Army, June 1917

35

PROPAGANDA AND CENSORSHIP

Propaganda is information or publicity put out by a government or organization to promote an idea or cause. During World War I propaganda was used by governments on all sides to encourage people at home to support the war.

A US poster invites the public to buy bonds to raise money for the fight against the Germans, represented by a demonic soldier.

US AND THEM

Propaganda encouraged patriotism – the love that people feel for their countries. And it demonized and mocked the enemy, portraying the other side in a bad light, especially following incidents in which the enemy had acted inhumanely. This helped to keep up morale and encouraged people to carry on the fight against the enemy.

YOUR COUNTRY NEEDS YOU

Propaganda also encouraged people to join the army, to work as nurses or in armaments factories, and to buy war bonds that would help the government to buy armaments.

PROPAGANDA AT THE FRONT

Propaganda did not only appear at home. It was common for propaganda leaflets to be dropped into enemy trenches. The leaflets often told soldiers that they had no chance of victory and encouraged them to put down their weapons.

FORMS OF PROPAGANDA

At the time of World War I, there was very little radio broadcasting and no television. Propaganda was spread by posters, leaflets, books, films and speeches. Newspapers were also used for propaganda, and were forced to print what a government wanted. Sometimes propaganda exaggerated the truth, and sometimes it was simply not true. It always played up good news from the war and played down bad news.

CENSORSHIP

Censorship worked alongside propaganda. It was designed to filter information so that people only found out what the government decided was safe for them to know. Censorship operated at the battlefront. Letters sent by soldiers to loved ones at home were checked to make sure they didn't give away any secrets about operations at the front, or talk about defeats in battle.

A US soldier makes use of time away from battle to pen a note to his family. His letter would have been checked to make sure it gave away no military secrets.

At home, newspapers were censored. Reports on the war were not allowed to mention exact places or names, as this could help the enemy. Anti-war propaganda was also stopped.

IN THEIR OWN WORDS

It is far better to face the bullets than to be killed at home by a bomb. Join the army at once and help to stop an air raid.

British propaganda poster

THE ZIMMERMAN TELEGRAM

The United States was keen to stay out of the war. But German espionage in the United States, such as the attack on Black Tom (see pages 14–15), together with broken German promises regarding submarine attacks, began to turn the United States against Germany. Then, in January 1917, a telegram arrived in the offices of the British 'Room 40' code-breakers (see page 25) that proved to be the final straw for the Americans.

TOP-SECRET MESSAGE

The telegram had been sent from Germany along Swedish-owned and US-owned telegraph lines. But these lines passed through Britain and were tapped. Two of the Room 40 team noticed that the message was encrypted using a complex cipher. This told them that the message must be top secret. Within hours they had deciphered some of the message. At first the code-breakers couldn't believe what they were seeing and thought they might have made a mistake. So, over the next few days, they deciphered the whole message to make sure they were right.

EXTRACT FROM THE TELEGRAM

'On the first of February, we intend to begin unrestricted submarine warfare. In spite of this, it is our intention to endeavor to keep the United States of America neutral. In the event of this not succeeding, we propose an alliance on the following basis with Mexico: that we shall make war together and make peace together. We shall give generous financial support, and an understanding on our part that Mexico is to re-conquer the lost territory in New Mexico, Texas, and Arizona.'

The telegram was from the German foreign minister, Arthur Zimmerman, to the German embassy in Mexico, and was addressed to the Mexican government. It suggested that Mexico should invade the United States, with military support from Germany. The Germans thought an attack from Mexico would deter the United States from entering the war in Europe. The British handed the deciphered telegram to US president Woodrow Wilson. Within weeks the United States had declared war on Germany. The Germans had scored a terrible own goal.

The Zimmerman Telegram, encrypted (below), and deciphered (right).

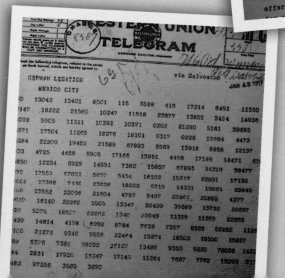

IN THEIR OWN WORDS

On 2 April 1917, US president Woodrow Wilson asked Congress to declare war on Germany. He said:

The world must be made safe for democracy. Its peace must be planted upon the tested foundations of political liberty.

39

THE HINDU-GERMAN CONSPIRACY

In 1914 India was part of the huge British Empire. Most Indians wanted independence from Britain. After Britain went to war with Germany, some radical Indians saw an opportunity to try and regain control of their country. They hatched a secret plot for a rebellion in India, which became known as the Hindu-German conspiracy.

Captain Franz von Papen, a German diplomat and military expert, who arranged a shipment of arms from the United States to India for use against the British.

THE CONSPIRATORS

Indians in different countries were involved in the conspiracy. Of course, there were nationalist Indians in India itself. But there was also the Ghadar Party, an organization of Indians in the United States dedicated to Indian independence. And there was the Indian Independence Committee, formed by Indian activists living in Germany. The conspirators were

THE NIEDERMAYER-HENTIG EXPEDITION

At the beginning of the war, Afghanistan, India's neighbour, was also under British rule. The Central Powers saw a chance to fight the British here, too. In 1915 they sent a secret expedition to Afghanistan, led by German army officers Oskar Niedermayer and Werner Otto von Hentig. The plan was to encourage Afghanistan to declare independence, join the Central Powers and attack the British in India. However, Niedermayer and Hentig could not persuade the Afghan leaders to act.

Despite the Hindu-German conspiracy, thousands of Indians fought on the Allied side during World War I. These are Indian machine gunners in action in Egypt.

supported by the German government, which was keen for British forces to be tied up fighting in India to give Germany an advantage on the Western Front.

THE PLOT

The conspirators' plan was to create a mutiny against British rule throughout India, especially in the ranks of the Indian army. Members of the Ghadar Party went to India from the United States. They began to spread propaganda, organize the nationalists in India and hold secret talks with members of the Indian army. They also arranged for weapons to be shipped from the United States. A date for the mutiny was set in February 1915. But British intelligence agents had discovered the plot, and, at the last moment, the leaders of the conspiracy were arrested.

IN THEIR OWN WORDS

After the plot was exposed, members of the Ghadar Party were tried in the United States. During the trial, the party's former president Ram Chandra was killed by a fellow defendant because he thought Ram Chandra was a British agent:

Ram Chandra arose and started across the room. Ram Singh also arose. He raised his revolver and began firing. Ram Chandra staggered forward and fell dead before the witness chair, with a bullet in his heart and two others in his body.

New York Times, April 1918

THE END OF THE WAR

As 1917 began, the war was in stalemate. Since 1914, the Western Front had moved no more than a few kilometres either way, despite major offences and millions of casualties. The story was the same on the Eastern Front, where the Russians and Germans were dug in.

A DECISIVE YEAR

Two major events of 1917 helped to bring the war to an end in 1918. First, in April, the United States entered the war on the Allied side and sent troops to Europe to help Britain and France. Secondly, the Russian Revolution began. The Russians were fed up with food and fuel shortages caused by the war. Eventually they revolted. The tsar of Russia was forced out, and in November a political group called the Bolsheviks seized power. The Bolsheviks started peace talks with Germany, and Russia withdrew from the war in March 1918.

World War I officially came to an end in November 1918, when generals of the Allied and Central powers signed the armistice on a train in France.

SECRETS OF WORLD WAR I

World War I was sparked by a secret plot by Serbs. Secret plots against the United States, which brought the United States into the war, helped to end it. Spies did not play a huge role in World War I, although they provided some useful information. However, codes and code-breaking did play a vital role. Without them, neither side could have operated at the battle front.

Jubilant crowds thronged the streets of British cities when news broke of the end of the war. Victory had been achieved and the survivors were on their way home from the battlefield.

In the autumn of 1918 the Allies, boosted by US forces, broke through the German lines. The Germans began to retreat. At the same time the German people at home were starving. A revolt against Kaiser Wilhelm II began when German sailors refused to take their warships to sea. The German government collapsed.

An armistice was agreed, and fighting stopped at 11 am on 11 November 1918. Germany was blamed for the war. It lost land in Europe and its colonies, and had to pay the victorious countries for the costs of the conflict.

COSTS OF THE WAR

World War I lasted four years and four months. In all, 10 million soldiers died, and 20 million were wounded. Vast areas of Belgium, France and Russia were devastated.

TIMELINE

June 1914 Archduke Franz Ferdinand, heir to the throne of Austria-Hungary, is assassinated by the Black Hand.

July 1914 Austria-Hungary declares war on Serbia, marking the start of World War I.

August 1914 Britain declares war on Germany; 21 suspect spies are arrested in Britain.

August 1914 The German *Magdeburg* code book is captured by the Russian navy.

September 1914 The first successful U-boat attack is made (against HMS *Pathfinder*).

April 1915 The Germans use poison gas on the battlefield for the first time.

May 1915 U-boat U-20 sinks the *Lusitania*.

October 1915 Edith Cavell is executed for helping trapped Allied soldiers escape through Belgium.

January 1916 The British Security Service, or MI5, is formed.

June 1916 Fritz Joubert Duquesne arranges the sinking of HMS *Hampshire*, killing British Secretary of State for War, Field Marshal Kitchener.

July 1916 German spies destroy Black Tom, a huge ammunitions depot near New York City.

September 1916 The British send tanks into battle for the first time.

January 1917 Zimmerman Telegram discovered by British 'Room 40' code-breakers.

April 1917 The United States enters the war.

June 1917 British tunnellers detonate 19 giant mines under the German lines in Belgium.

1918 The Germans introduce their ADFGX cipher for sending secret messages.

March 1918 Russia withdraws from the war.

November 1918 The Armistice is signed to bring World War I to an end.

GLOSSARY

alliance A group of countries fighting together on the same side.

Allied Powers or **Allies** The alliance between Britain, France and Russia during World War I.

armistice An agreement by opposing sides in a war to stop fighting.

assassination The killing of a political leader or public figure.

Balkans A collection of countries that makes up part of south-eastern Europe.

Central Powers or **Triple Alliance** The alliance between Germany, Austria-Hungary and other countries during World War I.

cipher A way of encrypting a message, where each letter in the message is changed into a different letter or group of letters.

code A way of encrypting a message, where words or phrases in the message are changed into groups of letters, numbers, signs or sounds.

code-breaker A person who tries to work out the meaning of intercepted coded messages.

counter-espionage Searching for enemy spies.

deported Forcibly removed from a country.

double agent A spy who appears to work for one side while actually working for the other.

encrypt Turn a message into a coded or ciphered form.

espionage Spying on and attacking the enemy in its own country.

grenade A bomb that is small enough to be thrown.

homing pigeon A pigeon trained to fly home to its nesting place from wherever it is released.

intelligence Information, often secret, about an enemy's forces and plans.

martyr A person killed because of his or her beliefs.

merchant ship Any non-military ship.

mine An explosive charge buried underground (or under the sea).

nationalist Supportive of the right of one's people to exist as a nation.

no-man's land The strip of land between the front lines of each side at the battlefront.

paranoid A state of extreme worry.

propaganda Information and publicity put out by a government to promote a policy, idea or cause.

reconnaissance Searching for and recording the positions of enemy forces.

sabotage The deliberate damaging or destruction of property or equipment.

spy ring A network of spies working together, passing information from an enemy country to home.

tap Connect a wire to a telephone or telegraph wire to listen into the signals going along the wire.

telegram A written message sent using Morse code over telegraph wires.

terrorist A person who uses violence to achieve political goals.

U-boat A German military submarine, especially one used during World Wars I and II.

war bonds Certificates sold to the public by governments to raise money for the war effort. War bonds were later repaid with interest.

FURTHER INFORMATION

BOOKS
Eyewitness: World War I
by Simon Adams (Dorling Kindersley, 2007)

The First World War
by Henry Brook, Rob Lloyd Jones and Conrad Mason
(Usborne, 2008)

Headlines of World War I
by Ken Hills (Evans, 2005)

Usborne True Stories: The First World War
by Paul Dowswell (Usborne, 2007)

Who? What? When? World War I
by Bob Fowke (Hodder, 2003)

WEBSITES
www.bbc.co.uk/history/worldwars/wwone
General information on World War I from the BBC's website

www.firstworldwar.com
Lots of information on the battles and soldiers of World War I

www.mi5.gov.uk/output/history.html
The history of MI5

www.nationalarchives.gov.uk/pathways/firstworldwar/index.htm
Information on World War I from the National Archives of the UK

www.sis.gov.uk/output/history-of-sis.html
The history of Britain's Secret Intelligence Service

INDEX

Page numbers in **bold** refer to pictures.

WORLD WAR I

CHRIS OXLADE

First published in 2010 by Franklin Watts

Copyright © 2010 Arcturus Publishing Limited

Franklin Watts
338 Euston Road
London NW1 3BH

Franklin Watts Australia
Level 17/207 Kent Street, Sydney, NSW 2000

Produced by Arcturus Publishing Limited,
26/27 Bickels Yard, 151–153 Bermondsey Street,
London SE1 3HA

The right of Chris Oxlade to be identified
as the author of this work has been asserted
by him in accordance with the Copyright,
Designs and Patents Act 1988.

Series concept: Alex Woolf
Editor and picture researcher: Alex Woolf
Designer: Tall Tree

A CIP catalogue record for this book is available from
the British Library.

Dewey Decimal Classification Number: 940.4'85

ISBN 978 0 7496 8230 9

Printed in China

Franklin Watts is a division of Hachette Children's
Books, an Hachette Livre UK company.
www.hachettelivre.co.uk

SL000974EN

This book belongs to

Faye Mayse.

Miss Mayse.

© JANE HISSEY 1987

For Cynthia Fitzjohn and her class
S.H.

For David and Elizabeth
T.G.

ACKNOWLEDGEMENTS

Every effort has been made to trace the ownership of all
copyrighted material and to secure the necessary permissions
to reprint these selections. In the event of any questions
arising as to the use of any material, the editor and the
publisher, while expressing regret for any inadvertent error,
will be happy to make the necessary correction in future printings.

Grateful acknowledgement is made to the following for
permission to reprint the copyrighted material listed below:

Pitman Publishing, London, for "Mouse in a Hole"
from NUMBER RHYMES AND FINGER PLAYS by Boyce and Bartlett.

Stainer & Bell Ltd for "Little Arabella Miller" by Anne Elliot
from FINGERS AND THUMBS. Reproduced by permission of Stainer & Bell Ltd.

The publisher would like to acknowledge the authors
of the following rhymes:
Mrs Wyn Daniel Evans for "Ten Galloping Horses",
Emilie Poulson for "The Beehive" and Christina Rossetti for "The Pancake"

First published 1988 by
Walker Books Ltd, Walker House, 87 Vauxhall Walk, London SE11 5HJ

This selection © 1988 Sarah Hayes
Illustrations © 1988 Toni Goffe

First printed 1988
Printed in Hong Kong by South China Printing Co.

British Library Cataloguing in Publication Data
Clap your hands: finger rhymes.
1. Finger play
I. Hayes, Sarah   II. Goffe, Toni
398'.8   FG1218.FS

ISBN 0-7445-0914-9

CLAP YOUR HANDS
FINGER RHYMES

Chosen by Sarah Hayes   *Illustrated by* Toni Goffe

CONTENTS

WALKER BOOKS
LONDON

Page 6

KNOCK AT THE DOOR

Knock at the door.   Peep in.   Lift the latch.   And walk in.

Chin chopper, chin chopper, chin chopper, chin.

HERE IS THE CHURCH

Here is the
church,

And here's the
steeple.

Open the
doors

I AM A COBBLER

I am a cobbler
And this is what I do:
Rap-tap-a-tap
To mend my shoe.

And here he is
Saying his
prayers.

And see all the
people.

Here is the parson
Going upstairs,

7

TWO FAT GENTLEMEN

Two fat gentlemen met in a lane,

Bowed most politely,

bowed once again.

How do you do,
How do you do,
And how do you do again?

Two thin ladies met in a lane,
Bowed most politely, bowed once again.
How do you do,
How do you do,
And how do you do again?

Two tall policemen met in a lane,
Bowed most politely, bowed once again.
How do you do,
How do you do,
And how do you do again?

Two little schoolboys met in a lane,
Bowed most politely, bowed once again.
How do you do,
How do you do,
And how do you do again?

Two little babies met in a lane,
Bowed most politely, bowed once again.
How do you do,
How do you do,
And how do you do again?

TEN GALLOPING HORSES

Ten galloping horses came through the town.

Five were white and five were brown.

They galloped up

and galloped down;

Ten galloping horses came through the town.

11

THE
BEEHIVE

Here is the beehive,
Where are the bees?
Hidden away where
nobody sees.

Soon they come creeping
Out of the hive.

One and two and three, four, five.

LITTLE MOUSIE

Here's a little mousie
Peeking through a hole.

Peek to the left.

Peek to the right.

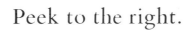

Pull your
head back in,

There's a
cat
in
sight!

MOUSE IN A HOLE

A mouse lived in
a little hole,

Lived softly in
a little hole,

When all was quiet
as quiet
can be...

OUT
POPPED
HE!

THREE LITTLE MONKEYS

Three little monkeys
Swinging from a tree,

Teasing Mr Alligator,
"Can't catch me!"

Along came Mr Alligator

Slowly as can be...

Then...

SNAP!

15

INCEY WINCEY SPIDER

Incey wincey spider
climbed up the water spout.

Down came the rain
and washed the spider out.

Out came the sun,
and dried up all the rain.

And incey wincey spider
climbed up the spout again.

16

CHOOK, CHOOK; CHOOK-CHOOK-CHOOK

Chook, chook; chook-chook-chook,

Good morning, Mrs Hen.

How many chickens have you got?

Madam, I've got ten.

Four of them are yellow,

And four of them are brown,

And two of them are speckled red —

The nicest in the town!

GOOD THINGS TO EAT

Will you have
a cookie,

Or a piece
of pie,

Or a striped
candy stick?

Well, so
will I.

THREE LITTLE PUMPKINS

Three little
pumpkins sitting
on a wall,

A witch
came
riding by—

Ha-ha-ha!
I'll take you all
To make a
pumpkin pie!

FIVE FAT PEAS

Five fat peas in a pea-pod pressed.

One grew,   two grew,   so did all the rest.

They grew   and did not   Until one day
and grew   stop,   the pod went POP!

TEN FAT SAUSAGES

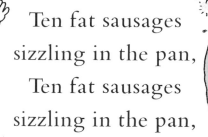

Ten fat sausages
sizzling in the pan,
Ten fat sausages
sizzling in the pan,

One went
POP

and another
went BANG.

There were eight fat sausages sizzling in the pan.

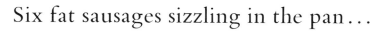

Eight fat sausages sizzling in the pan...

Six fat sausages sizzling in the pan...

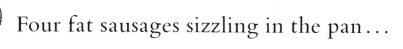

Four fat sausages sizzling in the pan...

Two fat sausages sizzling in the pan,
Two fat sausages sizzling in the pan,
One went POP and another went BANG.
There were no fat sausages sizzling in the pan.

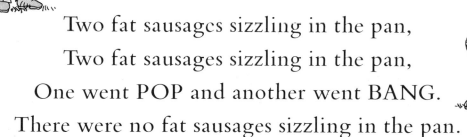

THE PANCAKE

Mix a pancake,
Stir a pancake,

Pop it in
the pan.

Fry the
pancake,

Toss the
pancake,

Catch it if you can.

PAT-A-CAKE

Pat-a-cake, pat-a-cake, baker's man,

Bake me a cake as fast as you can.

Pat it

and prick it,

and mark it with B,

And put it in the oven for Baby and me.

23

LITTLE TURTLE

There was a little turtle.

He lived in a box.

He swam in a puddle.

He climbed on the rocks.

He snapped at a mosquito.
He snapped at a flea.
He snapped at a minnow.
He snapped at me.

He caught the mosquito.
He caught the flea.
He caught the minnow.
But he didn't catch me.

ONE, TWO, THREE, FOUR, FIVE

One, two, three, four, five,

Once I caught a fish alive.

Six, seven, eight, nine, ten,

Then I let him go again.

Why did you let him go?
Because he bit my finger so.

Which finger did he bite?
This little finger on the right.

LITTLE ARABELLA MILLER

Little Arabella Miller
Found a woolly caterpillar.
First it crawled upon her mother,

Then upon her
baby brother.

All said,
"Arabella Miller,
Take away that
caterpillar!"

ROUND AND ROUND THE GARDEN

Round and round the garden, like a teddy bear;

One step,

two step,

Tickly under there!

IN A COTTAGE

In a cottage
in a wood

A little old man
at the window stood

Saw a rabbit
running by

Knocking
at the
window.

"Help me!
Help me! Help!"
he said,

"Lest the
huntsman shoot
me dead."

"Come little rabbit,
Come to me,
Happy you shall be."

HOW MANY

How many people live at your house?

One, my mother,

Two, my father,   Three, my sister,

Four, my brother.   There's one more,

now let me see.

Oh yes, of course. It must be me!